The Tao of Millennial Money, Second Edition

Disclaimer

This is a work of opinion and the information in this work is for educational and entertainment purposes only and does not constitute specific, individualized, or tailored financial advice in any way, shape, or form. No guarantee or warranty of any kind is associated with the information contained in this work. Please consult tax, financial, legal, or any other professional advisors you might consult, before considering following any of the ideas in this book.

Inspiration

I am writing this work without specifically referring to any other specific work on personal finance and investing. However, some of these bits of wisdom may resemble similar things others have suggested – but not on purpose. There are only so many ways to become financially free using legally available opportunities – for example, public markets (stocks, bonds, etc.), real estate, growing a business, etc. My goal is to repeat nothing that has been said before the exact same way in any other work but rather, to distill bits of financial wisdom into snippets of financial thinking that may be of benefit to the millennial generation. When I talk about people's need to have multiple streams of income, about the need to consider real assets, or buy assets, or think about passive income, these are my thoughts, inspired by reading and evaluating the concepts expounded in innumerous works by myriad authors, financial "gurus", and personalities. My heroes consist of those who can take their entrepreneurial drive and develop platforms that can change the world through cascading (serial) entrepreneurship. Names that further inspire my thinking in this regard are Richard

Branson, Jeff Bezos, and Elon Musk, although there are many, many others out there.

Dedication

This book is dedicated to *the Precariat*, a term I did not invent but which I feel continues to best describe the millennial generation. Born of hope for the future, educated in the life pathway of the second half of the 20th century, raised on social media, inheriting a rapidly changing world, imagining great possibilities in the decades ahead but existing in an ever more complex and precarious world of credit scores, rising costs, job insecurity, and stagnating wages that threatens personal financial calamity with the slightest of financial shocks. My hope is to reduce such risk by introducing concepts related to financial awareness and increase the *Precariat's* financial potential through knowledge and consideration of the macroeconomic environment.

Foreward (new in Second Edition)

One year since the first edition of this work was published and everything has changed – yet nothing has changed. The stock market has whipsawed violently between extreme highs and dramatic lows, the geopolitical environment remains cloudy and complicated, the domestic political environment remains cloudy and complicated, the weather is a mess (and cloudy and complicated), and in that years' time, more than a million college graduates have entered the workforce. The labor participation rate – the number of people working or looking to work – is roughly the same as it was a year ago. Yet, there is conflicting analysis of the current economy: the stock market is signaling recession and there are growing headwinds to economic growth and stability; yet, at the same time, the US federal reserve asserts that the economy is still strong, so strong that it can absorb additional interest rate hikes. The millennial generation is nearly completely through their college days and into the workforce, in one form or another.

Millennials, this book was written for you. While there are now board games that poke light at the plight of millennials (with one actually using a slogan that roughly translates into the idea that millennials should avoid thoughts about buying and making money in real estate since they can't afford it anyway). In reality, millennials have one big advantage over older generations: time. Millennials have their whole careers in front of them and they are now entering the age in which they will find jobs, or choose a career path, and start building their futures. More than anything, they have time. To borrow from the great American sport of football, it's not half-time for the millennials like it is for Generation X, or the fourth quarter like it is for the Baby Boomers. Nor is the game in overtime like it is for the Greatest Generation or even earlier generations.

Time is the greatest and most precious resource that exists in life. We can't make more, and we can't easily buy more - with the possible exception of lifesaving medical treatment. So how that time is spent makes a tremendous difference in our future lives. Just by reading this book, millennials are being exposed to thoughts and thinking about the future that could possibly lead to a more prosperous tomorrow. Prosperous in terms of financial success, of course, but that prosperity provides freedom of choice and opportunities to gave back to the less fortunate. Therefore, when millennials experience success financially, there is the potential for all to benefit. I see this as a great educational calling.

This book doesn't give a roadmap to riches. It doesn't tell you how you will find riches in your own life. There is no book, person, or advice, that can actually do that – to believe otherwise is fiction. However, there are ideas, ways of thinking, planning, that if considered earlier in life, may provide greater chances of success later. That's what this book represents: exposure to thoughts and ideas that could be useful. Only you can determine what will work for you – there are no guarantees here, or anywhere for that matter. But, in this work, I list ideas and thoughts that I think can save money, in some cases may make money, and occasionally, help one make more informed or smarter decisions financially.

This work is primarily focused on public asset classes. Why? They are easy to get into, relatively easy to get out of, and work well to illustrate basic concepts of using money to make money. Such investments include publicly-traded stock and bonds, CDs, bank accounts, real estate, commodities, and/or other more exotic investments that are semi-liquid (liquidity referring here to the ability to buy in or out of an investment). Side hustles can consist of a number of activities that produce additional income. There are innumerous and exotic investment opportunities that exist – these are beyond the scope of this book, as the intention here is to focus on asset classes that are generally available to early-career millennials and begin a thought process that considers best uses of capital than the expenditure of capital. Thought processes matter.

Here, revised and revisited, are a collection of wealth-related ideas. For a summary of more thoughts, ideas, and what I would do different if I could go back in time, be sure to read the Epilogue at the end of the work

Cal Kennedy, Jr.

December, 2018

A Full Bucket Begins with a Single Drop

Translation: Before you can make a lot of money, you must make "some money." Before you can define what "some money" means, you have to have something of value. Here let's term earning something of value as income. This means something with value (with worth) is *coming in*. When it comes to making money, saving money, investing money, everything matters – costs, fees, dividends, interest, money coming in and money going out. Understand that you can't get to be a millionaire without having a million dollars – technically, that's a million one dollar bills. Each of those dollar bills is 100 cents or 100 pennies worth of value. One penny less and a millionaire is no longer a millionaire.

Summary: When it comes to building wealth, every single penny/cent counts. Don't be afraid to start small. Snowball your wealth!

Begin Before the Sun Rises Again

Translation: The most important ally you have in investing is not how much you invest. It's time. More specifically, it's how long you can invest and grow wealth before you need to begin withdrawing from your accumulation. You can ready plenty of books and articles on the magic of time and compounding returns so there's no need to cover the nitty gritty details here. Suffice it to say, you can always potentially earn more money, and you can always potentially chase higher returns, but you'll never be able to create more time. At least not in the general sense. So use time to your advantage and start your financial wealth and investing strategy, no matter how small your account or restricted your after-tax income may be, today.

Summary: Don't wait to start investing or pursuing your financial well-being strategy. Even in the smallest amounts. You'll never get more time.

Cut the Grass When It Grows Too Fast

Translation: If you think of your investments as a carefully tended lawn, then if things go right, your investments will grow, just like a lawn would with water, sun, and care. Thus, just as would cut the grass when it gets too high and starts looking ragged, don't let your investment earnings grow too fast without cutting back and putting some of that money aside to use when the "grass" goes through a tough time (droughts happen!). People who get burned in public markets often fly too close to the sun, letting greed convince them that a growing investment will keep growing forever. Use hard-and-fast rules to frame your investing and to make profit-taking decisions. Think of your harvested profits as just that – sun, water, and care set aside to use when things go south – in technical terms, you should "rebalance" your investments to retain your risk tolerance. Doing so is one way to improve the odds that you'll keep the "lawn" looking great in the long term.

Imagine a pyramid make of bricks, where each brick represents a dollar of wealth. Many hope for a pyramid that keeps growing up, higher and higher. That is great, but it also means a lot of bricks can get toppled over if there is a storm or very strong winds. Instead, imagine taking some bricks from the top of the pyramid and using them to bolster and grow the base of the pyramid. The height of the pyramid after this process might be a little higher, but the base will certainly be wider. The goal is to grow the base as the height of the pyramid gets higher. In the end, ideally, one will have a much larger pyramid of wealth which will be much more stable due the effort expended in widening the base. Build your pyramid!

Summary: What goes up real fast tends to come down real fast. Especially in the world of public financial markets. A small profit is always better than a loss. Use profits to strengthen and inflate your overall wealth.

Don't Sell When the Market Stalls are Full

Translation: Markets don't go up forever. There will be times when the markets are tanking and all seems lost. The tendency for most people is to run for the exits. Panic and Sell! Panic and Sell! Why does everyone do this? Down markets are like a store putting good items on sale. Do you want to buy them when they are cheaper to purchase or when they are more expensive? Cheaper, of course! So, if you continue to believe in the value of your investments, then staying in the markets when the going gets tough, only investing what you can afford to lose, and harvesting your gains as mentioned previously makes more sense. Then, you'll be in a good place to buy again when things are cheaper and sell later when the markets recover. The 120+ year history of the US Stock Market shows that, although the time it takes to fully recover is different each time that there has been a "bear" market, the market has always eventually recovered from every historical crash!

The only exception to this concept is if the fundamentals of your investment choices have changed. If you invest in a company that later is revealed to be a criminal enterprise or Ponzi scheme or otherwise, then the fundamentals may have changed, and you may need to reevaluate whether continued investment is warranted.

Summary: If you've harvested gains ("cut the grass") and have money on the sidelines in reinvest-able cash, down markets can be a great time to buy. They are a terrible time to sell! The wait for markets to turnaround, however, is understandably difficult to stomach, and there are no future guarantees. However, the history of the US stock market over more than 100 years is that it has eventually always recovered after down periods.

Every Now and Then, A New Chapter Begins

Translation: Markets and particular investments don't tend to go up forever. Individual investments, whether stocks, bonds, commodities such as gold, or even real estate, can go up real fast, but they can also go down real fast too. Just ask people who bought real estate at the top of the market in 2006/2007. Or people who bought certain cryptocurrencies during the fall of 2017. Or the way things are looking in the stock market after a volatile 2018. There is a saying that I've heard from Wall Street giants, although I'm not sure who originally created the saying. It goes something like this: "You won't go broke making a profit." If you are lucky enough to own a hot investment, take some profit. If it keeps going up, you'll have made money to invest in other areas. If it goes down though, you'll be glad to have a profit to show for it. And then don't forget to reinvest some or all those gains, perhaps in a different asset class altogether. Analyze and evaluate your options and decide where your convictions lie.

Summary: The name of the game is "Buy Low and Sell High." I agree with the assertion made by some that Wall Street markets are indeed now a casino, thanks to information asymmetry, electronic trading algorithms, the proliferation of different and derivative investment mechanisms, and passive investing that can exacerbate price movement in both directions. Only those who can walk away from the table when they are ahead will be long-term winners.

Find Your Path and Follow It

Translation: Financial and investment advice is everywhere. You'll find all kinds of suggestions, mostly about investing in stocks and bonds, some about investing in commodities or real estate, others about alternative or exotic investments. What should you invest in? If you get into investing, over time, you're likely to find investments that you are interested in. You may dig in, take a deep dive, learn as much as you can and keep learning. Other people's investing advice is based on two things: 1) what has worked in the past and 2) what has worked for them. Find what works for you. And then become an expert in it. That expertise will increase your investing IQ. Read, read, and read. And don't stop learning about investing – increase your financial IQ!

Summary: Do your own research and pick the investments that you like and enjoy. You'll be a better investor for it.

Grass will Always Look Greener, Anywhere but Here

Translation: Markets don't rise or fall in tandem. Different sectors, different asset classes, different types of investments will be hot, others will be warm, and some will be cold. Market leaders change with time. One sector or asset class will look unstoppable – it's almost always an illusion. Money moves, especially big money. It doesn't like to stay in one place for a long time. As a small investor, as I assume most millennials, college students and recent college graduates reading this work are, you will suffer from information asymmetry compared the institutional and sovereign investment world. By the time many smaller investors move their money into the hot sector/asset of the time, that sector tends to lose funds and momentum as larger investors reallocate to new sectors that can be bought at a low price.

Summary: Be careful chasing returns. Investments that are too hot frequently leave small investors burned.

Have a parachute in reach, always

Translation: Most people make their money primarily from a job. However, the social contract of the mid-twentieth century, the lifetime job that was central to the American dream for decades, generally no longer exists in the first quarter of the 21st century. Even if it does exist somewhere, wage growth is uneven and income, even within the same occupation, is filled with inequality. Private organizations hire and fire employees at will, and for almost any reason desired. It is well-known that most extremely successful people do not make their income from one job – rather they frequently have multiple streams of legitimate income. Some have second jobs, some have hobbies that supply small amounts of income, some invest, some are in real estate, some have blogs, some develop websites, some receive royalties. Find a way to gain a second stream of income in addition to gainful employment or other form of occupation, no matter how small this stream begins. And then deploy it wisely. Realize that the traditional model of a job, followed by a comfortable retirement, and affordable healthcare looks as out of out date as horse-drawn carriages as a primary transportation source.

Summary: Expand your income potential. Begin pursuing a second line of income, no matter how small, today. And then start working on another line of income when the first one starts producing. Is it sad that primary employment frequently no longer pays enough to build steadily gaining wealth? Yes. Is it sad that people frequently need a side hustle to increase their income? Yes. But know that the option exists for those willing to work more for more income and it's almost a requirement in the modern economy to get ahead.

It's A Fool's Errand to Time Feelings

Translation: When the crash or correction in an investment or group of investments begins, the most sophisticated sell first. The less sophisticated stick things out until they reach a point where the loss is too great to bear and then they frequently sell at a significant loss. The most unsophisticated investors wait and wait during a correction, thinking that things will go back up, and will return to the value they were before the correction began. They tend to wait until it looks like their investments will keep going down forever. Sometimes, they throw in the cards and sell, just when everything looks terrible. Which is usually when the market begins to turn around – and when they have sold at such a great loss that recovery back to even is unlikely, at least in the near term. Research shows, time and time again, that humans are terrible at predicting markets and market timers are more wrong than they are right. No one can reliably time markets. Keep in mind that market swings are strongly affected by how people feel, and investor psychology can never truly be predicted with certainty in advance.

Summary: Avoid trying to time markets and use sound judgement and/or logic rules to make your investment decisions. No one can time the markets accurately, all of the time, and no one has a reliable crystal ball.

Jump in When the Water is Cool

Translation: Once upon a time, baseball cards were hot. I mean scorching hot. People made and lost fortunes of real money buying and selling mass-produced cardboard relics. The people that made the money were the people that had old or increasingly in-demand cardboard with the names of well-known stars on the front. The people that lost money were the people like me that bought a Jose Canseco rookie card for $120 US dollars in 1990 and watched it depreciate to $25 US dollars by 2010.

Such market stories happen over and over. As they say, history rhymes. When it comes to individual investments, there is a time when things are heating up and the time to buy is right. There is also a time when things are too hot or conversely, when things are too cold. Finding diamonds among common rocks is not easy. But it can be done. Use megatrends to your advantage and conduct your own research into areas/things that you anticipate will be increasing in demand with time.

What areas of the economy do you think will be hot over the next decade or so?

Summary: Timing markets is a sucker's game and hindsight is always 20/20. Doing research and finding fundamental reasons for an investment to increase in demand is a much stronger strategy.

Keep Cutting the Cords that Bind

Translation: One nearly certain way to lose money in the long run is to have a high level of expenses. This is as true in life as it is in investing. It's easy to spend money. There's no skill required. It's harder to spend money wisely. And harder still is earning it. Hardest of all is making it without earning it, since money made with investments is not considered "earned" for tax purposes – it's money making more money. Reduce the expenses that are associated with your investments. Try not to use high cost brokers, save on transaction costs wherever possible, and if using mutual funds, ETFs, or other expense-generating investments, focus in on costs and minimize these wherever possible. There are brokers out there that have free investment accounts and free trading of (albeit limited) investment opportunities. Research your options to save today, tomorrow, and for as long as you invest.

While you focus on cutting investment costs, keep cutting all other costs. This includes revolving and fixed costs. Always explore ways to cut costs further.

Summary: Investment costs can be a significant drag on your profit potential, much more than you might think. Minimize wherever possible and never invest without considering these outflows.

Living Well is More About What Leaves Than What Comes In

Translation: Everything that matters financially in life is about expenses. If you want to be rich, why is that? So that you can afford to live the life that you want, pursue the passions that you enjoy with the time that you have on this earth? Help others live their ideal life? Why do you need to work to make money, or need more money, or want to invest to make a lot more money? Is it because the things you want to do, or the lifestyle you want costs a lot? If so, then it's the cost holding you back, not the money you have. Want to live in a mansion with an oceanfront view? It costs a lot. What if it cost only a little? What if all the things you wanted or were passionate about cost only a little? I can't guarantee that you can get exactly what you want for a lot less, but most things (housing, health care, education, food, entertainment, you name it) can be found for less than you might imagine, sometimes a lot less, and usually somewhere else. Realize that you make a choice everyday – to keep living the life that you've arranged for yourself. Know that the world is filled with opportunities, but they come at a cost other than just money. Organize your life around minimizing expenses, whatever they are and wherever you are, so that you can get more out of life.

Cut your expenses to the bone. If you want to splurge, then splurge, if you can afford it. But if you cut your costs to the bare minimum, make more money, reduce debt, and invest, you can be on the path to a solid financial future.

Summary: You'll never be rich enough if you buy into escalating prices. You'll be part of the "it's never enough" crowd and trapped in the "rat race" forever. Gain control of your expenses and costs first and foremost. When you find that you're in a hole, don't keep digging!

Money Will Be Your Boss, If You Let It

Translation: Most people fall into the trap of working to make payments to someone else – a bank for their mortgage, financial companies for credit cards, the doctor, the hospital, the insurance company, the electronics store, and on and on. Not to mention paying a significant chunk of change first to the IRS and state or local governments for a cut of all wages and income. Many of these expenses could be reduced (even in the case of taxes, reduced legally). I find Robert Kiyosaki's books most inspirational on the topic of breaking out of the rat race, but read up on making your money work for you from as many sources as you can and then start working on making it happen. Start today. This is a marathon, not a sprint.

Summary: Debt and owing is a double-edged sword. When used for growth potential (education, sometimes real estate, sometimes starting a business) it can cut through the fog and open opportunities. When used for dumb purposes, like buying unnecessary junk, it can cut you to pieces.

Never Confuse the Wedding for the Marriage

Translation: Nothing, and I mean nothing, causes people to open their purse-strings like an emotional event such as a wedding (or numerous other emotion-based activities). Budgets are frequently blown out of the water for a half-day (or less) party. I mean, the dress, the entertainment, the decorations, the food, the photographer, the venue, the planner, the cake…you get the point. Emotion frequently overrides common sense and people spend absurd amounts of money for these things. Plus, rings, a honeymoon, and a host of other overpriced wedding-associated costs. Why do so many people get divorced? A lot of them confuse a wedding with a marriage, becoming so focused on the celebration that they may not really know the person that they are marrying. And I'm especially talking to millennials, college-aged and recent college graduates. Sure, there are some exceptions, but if you're in your early-to-mid-twenties, you probably have no real idea what you want out of life or what you really need in a partner, even if you think you do. No need to rush into marriage (especially, just to have a wedding and get a dress).

Marriage is an economic and social contract. It is not a declaration of love. Love doesn't require a ceremony or material goods. Be smart about wedding planning, never confuse a party with a lifetime of occasional ups and many (many) downs, and for the love of all this is holy in the universe, never, ever go into debt for a wedding.

Summary: A wedding is not an investment. It is a party that you throw for everyone else if you are the one getting married. You can still have a great time and a party without going into debt to do it. I don't understand how people can spend $20,000+ or more on a wedding and go into extended debt to do it. Do you really want to spend your shiny new married life paying off wedding debt for the next 10 years or longer? Or depleting retirement accounts to do so?

Only Growth Gets One Above the Thicket

Translation: There is a lot of financial advice out there on what to do if you have debt but want to invest. The advice is all over the place. Some say pay off all debt before investing. Others say pay off high interest debt before investing. Still others say split your money between paying off debt, saving, and investing. Since there's so much advice out there, let me throw in my opinion as well. I believe that our society depends on continual spending for economic success. The majority of jobs and businesses depend on consumer spending, aka consumption. So, although there are extreme savers who can resist this temptation to spend, invest nearly all of their income and retire at age 30, you'd probably not be reading this book if you were one of them. I also don't think a life of ramen noodles, recycling newspaper to use as toilet paper, and trapping squirrels for stew is necessary in the wealthiest country that has ever existed. I believe that some money must go towards growing wealth no matter how much you owe. This does not mean that you should not pay off debt. It means that you should be saving and investing while paying off debt. Yes, it may take longer to pay that debt off. However, I believe that spending behavior is largely set by the mid-20's and the most important factor in investment success is time. You can always try to make more money – you'll never be able to get back time that was lost, and the compounded returns your investments or wiser spending choices could have provided.

Summary: Don't choose between paying off debt and investing. Do both. And stop getting further in debt.

Prepare for Turbulence in Advance

Translation: Newsflash for millennials – life is difficult. No matter how great or miserable the current day, things change, sometimes for the better, but sometimes for the worse. One way to have more freedom of choice when things go south is to earn more, make more from your investments, and reduce expenses (including expenses involving debt). When one gets into investing, obviously, the goal is to have great returns, great growth, and increased wealth. However, always remember that good markets go bad every so often, hot sectors rotate, and money moves. No market stays hot forever without experiencing some hiccups.

There are some investments that are considered safety assets. There are many different types of investments that qualify for this term, but one example frequently touted is gold, although there are many others depending on whose advice you are receiving. Most experts recommend having some investments in such safety assets, but only a small component of one's investment portfolio. The goal of such investments is not necessarily to achieve great returns – actually, I am not sure it is right to really call them investments. Their purpose is to serve as insurance by theoretically providing a positive return (or holding value) when other assets are going down and dropping in value. Just as you wouldn't spend all of your money on conventional insurance, don't spend too much money on safety assets. Most experts recommend something like 4-6% of portfolio (a collection of investments) assets invested for safety/insurance purposes, but only you can determine what percentage of safety assets helps you sleep at night.

Summary: Safety assets act as insurance in a collection of investments. Most experts recommend having some safety assets but not more than a few percent of the total amount invested as a general rule-of-thumb. Read as much as you can about "safe haven" investments.

Question All Free Financial Advice

Translation: There is a lot of free financial advice out there. News channels frequently have financial websites that offer articles and blog entries from "experts" on how to easily save more money, how to easily save for a down-payment, how to easily live on $10 a week, the need to have a safety net of 3-6-12-24 months of expenses, and so on. Also, how to turn a $5 a week investment into a million dollars in 50 years. Most of these articles and reports are absurd and treat readers as if they are 8-year olds. Articles that tell you how to save an extra $500 dollars a week and such are useless and generalized beyond reality. If you had an extra $500 per week, you'd probably be saving it already! The ones that tell you you're not saving enough and need to squeeze blood from a stone and save more are also insulting. They generally provide no actual details on how to do this, beyond the typical "stop drinking that daily expensive coffee from the expensive coffee store" or "don't eat lunch out" advice. Or, go get a side hustle or two because your full-time job, which busts your ass all day long, doesn't pay enough to actually accomplish any goals that involve building wealth and moving ahead. One option is to find a way to make more money from your investments to cover eating those lunches out and having that coffee so you don't have to pursue three side gigs when you're young and relatively healthy. Life is short, better smell the flowers while you can. Motivate yourself to find a way to cover these splurges with your newfound interest in investing – it can be done. In addition, that expensive coffee that you can't give up might lead to more productivity at work than would otherwise be the case, potentially generating opportunities that might not exist if you avoided that caffeine jolt altogether. In addition, question any advice about owning any specific investments, such as individual stocks and bonds, etc.

Summary: Do your own investment research and make your own decisions. Most free financial advice is less than useless and in some cases, potentially psychologically harmful. No one can promise you an easy path, but by starting to think about your financial health, you've started down a path that can lead to economic stability.

Real Estate Means Forever

Translation: There's a lot of advice out there on the American dream. Supposedly, it involves a house (and perhaps a fence and some grass and so on...). However, the situation with real estate from a value perspective is not so simple as it once was. Homes are no longer constructed the way they once were, handcrafted with solid wood materials, real stone, crafted brick, and with an eye for detail. Modern homes are frequently mass constructed, using cheap labor, flimsy materials like OSB and plywood, under-insulated, and with poor fit and finish. The goal is frequently get the housing up and get it sold, much less than do it right. Of course, there are exceptions, but these are rare and generally custom (which means expensive). And that can mean more maintenance costs, a lot more. Add to that the myriad of costs associated with home ownership: a mortgage; HOA fees that can be exorbitant; community fees that are similar to, but in addition to, property taxes; yard and exterior maintenance that never ends, and as usual, property taxes. In most places in the US, property taxes are forever. In the few places where property tax phases out with age or exemption, they phase back in for the next owner. This illustrates the fundamental truth of real estate, as defined by many other financial experts: real estate does not mean "real" as in tangible. I have read so many authors who have discussed this but I think Robert Kiyosaki defined this in a way I would never forget: the word "real" in "real estate" is an alliteration of the Spanish work for royal – reale. The government owns all land, forever. Buying real estate is really a lease with a different name as property taxes are due annually, and if not paid, such land and homes on it can be repossessed – even if you've paid off your home! These issues and many other economic pitfalls have many millennials shunning home buying and focused on renting to keep their options open. Moreover, many millennials must move where the jobs are, sometimes frequently. This is not easy to do if one must sell a home where they are now to take a job where they need to be later. Although I do believe that carefully-considered real estate can be part of an overall wealth building strategy, I don't think it is wise to just blanketly consider any real estate purchase as an investment. Instead, why not focus on its utility as a place to live from a price and time perspective? Finally, as many people saw during the great recession, one could be halfway through paying off a mortgage and still lose their homes to foreclosure once they fall further and further behind on payments. Buying a house with a mortgage is voluntarily taking on great risk over a very long term and in my mind, is equivalent to indentured servitude.

Summary: I've bought houses and I've rented. Renting is better for freedom. Buying is better for living and customizing. Both come with significant advantages and disadvantages. Tread very carefully and thoughtfully in this space.

Spending is the Death of Possibility

Translation: Every time you make a purchase, consider wants and needs. Needs should have priority. Remember that wants are unlimited and there are millions of ways to go broke. Like spending money on stupid things. For example, many financial authors recommend that you never purchase luxuries. Luxuries are an example of a diminishing return good – you pay a lot more for them, but get little, if any, functional improvement over lesser-priced but well-made goods. Remember that once you've spent money, all the possibilities for what that money could have been used for are gone. Think about that each time you want to spend – is it worth it? And not just from a price perspective.

If you are going to spend, and you know that you have the discipline to follow and stick to a plan, then my suggestion is to explore using whole life insurance strategies to create an infinite banking loop. These types of plans go by many names, including infinite banking, banking on yourself, etc. They are not scams, get rich-quick schemes, or ways to suddenly win the lottery. They are legitimate methods of building long-term wealth while being able to access it without the typical penalties in governmental retirement-oriented plans. However, they do require discipline and commitment to work correctly. Many financial pundits think most people don't have the commitment to stick to these plans and argue against them for other reasons, including commissions. The reality is that the effectiveness of these plans depends on the age and health of the individual, the amount of coverage desired, the type of plan chosen, and the characteristics of the company they are using, and the commitment to stick to a plan.

Summary: There is an opportunity cost to spending money. That money could have been used for other opportunities. Explore infinite banking-type plans to see if they make sense for you. These plans are cheaper and more effective the younger and more healthy one is when the plan is initiated.

The Thousand Mile Journey Begins with a Single Step

Translation: If you have bad spending habits, as most U.S. consumers do, start working on them now. Here is the human condition – wants will always exceed needs and both will always exceed available resources (for example, money) depending on how needs are defined individually. Wants are infinite. Therefore no one is ever satisfied – people with aspirations to be rich want to be millionaires, millionaires want to be billionaires, billionaires want to keep increasing their wealth, and so on.

Summary: Read, study, and understand the difference between making money, saving money, spending money, and growing money. Start making more, saving more, and growing more today. Not tomorrow.

Use Every Tool in the Workshop

Translation: Pay less for everything. Take advantage of every opportunity to save money on purchases and spending. Consider using the money saved toward investments. How? Use every option to save, such as loyalty programs, points on any credit cards owned, online rebate programs, coupons, sales, you name it. For example, one might put all of their monthly utility bills (phone, energy, water, cable, internet) on a charge (not credit) card – one which requires that the owner has to pay off the balance of new charges each month. Since one must pay these charges each month no matter what, by putting them on a rewards charge card that must be paid off each billing cycle, that individual can automatically rack up reward points. Sometimes there is a sale on the number of points for a gift card, so they can then save when they get the gift card. Then that individual could find an online sale on an item that they would like to purchase, and go through the portal of an online rebate consolidator to make the purchase of that item at an already discounted price. They could then receive a certain percentage of cash back that comes in the form of a check when they've earned the minimum necessary. Be creative and be smart about every purchase, and cascade your savings potential. This will force you to think about what you're buying, if you really need it, and if so, how to get it for less and earn "found money" that can be invested or used to pay down debt. Make it a game, but don't "go broke saving money", as the saying goes.

Summary: Make no mistake, this is not a strategy for making money. This is a strategy for spending less money when a purchase is necessary. And my suggestion is to take the proceeds of any savings and invest half and pay down debt with the other half.

Value is More Important than Price

Translation: When considering a purchase, do not look at just the price in dollars and cents. Value is the most important parameter! If you buy something that has a low cost, but it must be replaced frequently, or doesn't work as intended, then it also has low value. In the case of luxuries, as mentioned earlier, the value proposition is generally negative – you pay a lot more and get little more in return. In other cases, however, you may pay a lot less, but get a piece of junk in return that quickly breaks, wears out, looks bad, or fits poor. Look for options that have the best value. Save every dollar that you can and buy based on value, not just price. Do a due diligence procedure for every purchase that you can.

Summary: Use every free resource on the value of products to help with decision making. Be careful to avoid or be skeptical of paid reviews which may not reveal true value!

Whole is Better than Half

Translation: If you are a millennial, or headed into the college-aged cohort, or even if you are under-40 and left school and late-nights behind a while ago, life insurance is probably not something you think about a lot. But you should think about it now. Maybe you already have a family to look out for, or maybe you are waiting for the right person to come along. Life insurance is something to think about when you are ready to retire, right? Wrong. Life insurance is something to think about when you are young and healthier than you will be later in life. Unless you find the fountain of youth and never age. For the rest of us, death is a certain consequence of being alive. Think about helping those who will still be here when you have gone ahead. More importantly, and especially if you are using a group term life policy offered as a benefit at your job, do your due diligence now and explore whole life insurance options from different mutual insurance companies. Yes, they cost far more that term policies. But the right policies build cash value that can be used when you are alive, for many purposes. Whole life might not be right for you, and any such policies should be part of a financial plan, not the entirety of it. But explore the possibilities today – there are only two ways I know of to grow after-tax money on a tax-deferred basis and *use* – not necessarily withdraw – these funds tax-free: Roth IRAs and properly structured, dividend-paying Whole Life (sometimes called 7702) policies.

Summary: Nobody in the financial services industries has a vested interest in promoting whole life policies if they only sell financial products for 401(k) or IRA or taxable accounts. In fact, responses are usually downright hostile against these whole life policies. If you find negative information on whole life, see if that information is coming from an investment company. Learn about the infinite banking-type concept today, and see if it is worth considering. Every day that goes by is a day that will cost more if you decide to include this strategy that combines life insurance and an investment component in your portfolio. Remember that whole life insurance includes options for use during the living years; term life insurance like that offered through most workplaces is death insurance.

Xtra Attention to Yourself Pays Certain Dividends

Translation: Have you ever heard the saying that "Health is Wealth"? While many people can certainly achieve material wealth and fame independently of any disability, the road to financial independence is made much more difficult for someone in poor health. Health issues require attention, which can require time and energy away from the issues associated with attaining an upward career trajectory and increased compensation, the lynchpin of the human capital-based (e.g., work-based) 20th-century American Dream. The most successful people are healthy, or at least, can meet the mental and physical energy demands and frenetic pace that upward mobility demands. Taking care of oneself is an investment in a good life, in possibilities, and in a payoff for deferred gratification. If you are engaging in self-harmful behavior (binge drinking, smoking, or illicit drug use), stop these activities now, or accept that you will never rise above the crowd and that this book is likely of no use to you. These things are likely to shorten your life and they will certainly divert money from your bank account and investments into brief minutes of entertainment that will leave you empty and anticipating the next buzz. I have no preference for a particular diet or exercise regimen. Just start to think about what you are eating, especially chemical-loaded or processed junk, and start to reduce your intake of such material. Similarly, I am not a big fan of marathons – just getting up and getting active in something, even occasionally, is better than nothing. Movement is life, and eating right encourages movement.

Summary: Start taking care of your health now…like yesterday. You can always try to earn more money if you are healthy. You can never get more time or turn back the clock, and it's a lot harder to get healthy again once wellness has been lost.

You don't Get a Second Act in American Life

Translation: To paraphrase one of F. Scott Fitzgerald's most famous lines, the true meaning of which is still debated today. I think Fitzgerald was on to an observation, but I believe that each of us can define it in our own way. In my opinion, Fitzgerald was trying to emphasize how important it is to be careful. Be careful in the jobs you select, in your choice of a significant other, in your relationships with people and with money. If you ruin your reputation, you may not be able to recover completely, in one sense or another. If you ruin your credit, you may be able to recover somewhat, over a period of years, but there can be an opportunity cost to years of credit damage, unfortunately (even though I think it would be better for all if we didn't depend on credit for continued consumption). There are frequently exceptions to generalizations, and there are people that have fallen on hard times and come out ahead in the end. But these stories are exceptions, which mean they are not the rule. Now, while you are young, begin to view the life ahead as a marathon, the goal of which is to cross the finish line – which every individual must define in their own way. One must both survive, but also use logic, skill, and luck to thrive along the way. Everyone makes mistakes, but some mistakes are much more challenging to overcome, so think about the path to come and take steps to minimize the risk of making financial mistakes.

Summary: Life is hard enough as it is, and it's only getting more complicated. Think about your future today, and know that you may have more control over your financial future than any other aspect of your life.

Zero is the Loneliest Number

Translation: Think of all the different ways in which you could deploy your capital, your income, your money. Some of those ways involve spending, and the loss of your capital forever. Others involve ways to turn a dollar of capital into two dollars, and two dollars into four dollars, and so on. Are you invested? Do you have opportunities that you have not taken advantage of to increase or build wealth? Those opportunities are currently providing you zero dollars in benefits or income. Do your due diligence, decide which path you think you would like to pursue, and then act. Time is literally running out.

Summary: Ideas and opportunities not acted upon will always remain unfulfilled dreams. Do your research, and then take a calculated risk. Or be satisfied with the likelihood that nothing will change.

The View from the Top of the Mountain

Translation: Everyone has their own goals in life. Financial freedom and more money don't always achieve those goals, but financial freedom does provide one important advantage: opportunity. Opportunity to spend time how one pleases, whether productively or otherwise, including having time to do nothing. Each person has their own mountain to climb to achieve their version of success. Some mountains will be taller than others. There will be more people at the bottom and at lower elevations than at the top, but many people – if not everyone – will be trying to climb higher. I encourage you to use your success, as you climb your mountain to whatever height you aspire to, to help others on their way up. Find a way to leverage your success to help them and society. Leave this world in a better place than where it was when you entered it. Working together, we can make a difference for good. Start now. If you cannot afford to donate money, find a way to donate some time, which is generally more effective in any case. Every minute spent helping a good cause makes this world a better place.

Summary: I hope that you will use these tiny bits of wisdom to improve your financial life, even if only minimally. My only request is to leverage your success, however large or small, to help this world and the people in it in some respect. I hope you can summit your own mountain, however high it is.

Epilogue

The world is on fire. Millennials, I don't blame you one bit for looking out at the world of chaos and deciding to focus on fun experiences, escapes, ways to save money such as ride or home sharing, utilizing social media and technology in their daily life experiences, and frequently working two or more jobs to make ends meet. It's not getting easier. And the complete pandemonium of our elected representatives, consequences of globalization, and oligopolistic nature of modern capitalism isn't helping. But the sooner one explores alternatives, the sooner something can be done to improve future possibilities.

This work tries to provide financial talking points to get one started in thinking about moving ahead and building wealth and financial health. From here, I suggest that one read no less than one financial work per month from here on out. Building your financial IQ is essential to your overall long-term success.

What would I do differently if I could go back in time and do things differently?

1) Invest in an IRA from the very first day that I was eligible. I like non-deductible Roth IRAs because once the qualifications are met, income is federally tax-free, but there are other types of IRAs, including the traditional IRA that is tax-deductible.

2) I would have opened a dividend-paying whole life insurance policy as an infinite banking strategy for as high a face value as I could afford at the shortest non-MEC payoff possible. (MEC is something you want to avoid if opening an infinite banking type policy).

3) I would have stayed at jobs offering a pension for long enough to minimally vest in the pension plan. I would use the IRA for market exposure, pension for high-confidence benefits, and optionally contribute to a 401k-type plan just enough to reach the company match.

4) After my first job out of school, I would stay at any place of employment for no less than three years. I feel that people can explain an initial work experience that lasted a year or less as long as that leads to a better position or one with greater potential for advancement. However, I think job-hopping is still an issue that is associated with red flags, and three-to-five years is a better time frame to aim for in each job.

5) I would have used educational benefits to the max. Not only to pursue additional degrees, but even for individual courses, training, or foreign language learning development. If you have the opportunity to use educational benefits through employment, I suggest using them to the greatest extent possible. Never stop learning – learning is growth!

It is a brave new world. Then again, it always has been, for every new generation. I hope that you will achieve your definition of success. Remember, life is a marathon, not a sprint. Plan your route. And follow your plan.

www.ingramcontent.com/pod-product-compliance
Lightning Source LLC
Chambersburg PA
CBHW030551220526
45463CB00007B/3060